Monkeys Sticker Book

Laura Howell

Illustrated by John Francis

About this book

This book is about monkeys and other hairy animals called primates, which have grasping fingers and good eyesight. Monkeys are the biggest group of primates, and are themselves split into two groups, New World and Old World, depending on where they live.

Although it's called the Monkeys Sticker Book, because there are lots of monkeys in it, this book also includes information about the other kinds of primates, which are called prosimians and apes.

The measurements given for the animals are averages. The length is measured without the tail.

If the male and female look very different, both are shown. These symbols show which animal is which.

Abbreviations are used in some place names: N(orth), E(ast), S(outh), W(est), C(entral).

Old World monkeys

Old World monkeys live in Africa and Asia, in forests and mountain areas or on open ground. They mostly eat leaves and fruits. All Old World monkeys have forward-pointing nostrils, and most have a tail.

Talapoin

Vervet monkey

Vervets use unique alarm calls to warn each other of different enemies, such as owls and snakes. 35-66cm (13¾-26in) S and E Africa

WHEN ....

WHERE ....

Vervet monkey

Talapoin

Talapoins are the smallest of the Old World monkeys. They are good swimmers and usually live near water. 32-45cm (12½-17¾in) Angola, Zaire

WHEN ....

WHERE ....

Patas monkey

Allen's swamp monkey

As its name suggests, this monkey lives in swamp forests. Its toes and fingers are slightly webbed, which helps it to swim. 45-51cm (17¾-20in) DR Congo, Zaire

WHEN ....

WHERE ....

Allen's swamp monkey

Patas monkey

Patas monkeys can move at speeds of up to 55kph (34mph), making them the fastest runners of all the primates. Up to 85cm (33½in) W and E Africa

WHEN ....

WHERE ....

Pig-tailed macaque

Intelligent, nimble monkeys that can be trained by people to climb trees and gather fruit for them. They are so-named because of their short, slightly curled tails. 43-77cm (17-30$^{1}/_{4}$in) SE Asia

WHEN ....

WHERE ....

Pig-tailed macaque

Lion-tailed macaque

Like a lion, this macaque has a tufted tail. Its mane of light hair stands out dramatically from its dark body. 51-61cm (20-24in) India (endangered)

WHEN ....

WHERE ....

Lion-tailed macaque

Celebes crested macaque

Celebes crested macaque

Also called Sulawesi crested macaques. These monkeys have tall hair tufts, long faces and bald bottoms. 45-60cm (17$^{3}/_{4}$-23$^{1}/_{2}$in) Indonesia (critically endangered)

WHEN ....

WHERE ....

Stump-tailed macaque

Stump-tailed macaque

Also called bear macaques, because of their shaggy fur and bear-like shape. Babies have white hair which darkens with age. Older monkeys have dark faces. 48-65cm (19-25$^{1}/_{2}$in) SE Asia, S China

WHEN ....

WHERE ....

Old World: baboons & mandrills

Hamadryas baboon

Hamadryas baboons were sacred to the Ancient Egyptians, although none live in Egypt today. Males have a "cape" of long, silver fur. Females are smaller, with short, brown fur. Up to 76cm (30in) NE Africa

WHEN ....

WHERE ....

♀ Hamadryas baboon ♂

Olive baboon

Olive baboon

Also called the Anubis baboon. This is the most widespread baboon species, found in 25 countries. It takes its name from the olive-green tinge of its fur. 60-90cm (23½-35½in) Equatorial Africa

WHEN ....

WHERE ....

Gelada baboon

Geladas have a distinctive hourglass-shaped patch of bare skin on their chest. On females, this brightens and swells to show when she is ready to breed. Males have a tufted tail and fur "cape". 50-74cm (19¾-29in) Ethiopia

WHEN ....

WHERE ....

Gelada baboon

Mandrill

Mandrill

Mandrills are the largest monkey species. You can easily recognize males by the bright markings on their face and rump. They bare their huge fangs to threaten enemies. Up to 80cm (31½in) C Africa

WHEN ....

WHERE ....

Drill

Drill

Drills are very similar to mandrills, but with duller facial markings. Males are much larger than females, and have blue and mauve rumps. Up to 70cm (27½in) C Africa

WHEN ....

WHERE ....

White-collared mangabey

Also called the sooty mangabey. Mangabeys are medium-sized, baboon-like monkeys. Look for the "collar" of white fur around its face. Up to 62cm (24½in) Africa

WHEN ....

WHERE ....

White-collared mangabey

Kipunji

Also called the highland mangabey. Experts have found that kipunjis look and behave like mangabeys, but are closely related to baboons. Up to 1m (3¼ft) Tanzania (critically endangered)

WHEN ....

WHERE ....

Kipunji

Old World: colobus monkeys

Zanzibar red colobus

Like all colobus monkeys, this boldly marked animal has long fingers and limbs for swinging through the treetops, but only tiny stubs for thumbs. 45-65cm (17¾-25½in) Zanzibar (endangered)

WHEN ....

WHERE ....

Zanzibar red colobus

King colobus

The king colobus has a dark body with a bright white tail, and straggly white hair on its face and chest. 55-70cm (21½-27½in) W Africa

WHEN ....

WHERE ....

King colobus

Eastern black and white colobus

Eastern black and white colobus

Also called a mantled guereza. Adults have tail tufts and striking black and white markings. Babies are all white. 45-71cm (17¾-28in) Equatorial Africa

WHEN ....

WHERE ....

Olive colobus

Olive colobus

The smallest type of colobus. Females carry their young in their mouths, instead of letting them cling to their bellies like most primate mothers. 38-50cm (15-19¾in) Africa

WHEN ....

WHERE ....

Old World: leaf monkeys

Hanuman langur

Hanuman langur

Hanuman langurs are named after a heroic monkey warrior in the Hindu religion. 40-75cm (15³/₄-29¹/₂in) Asia

WHEN ....

WHERE ....

Dusky leaf monkey

Dusky leaf monkey

Also called a spectacled langur, because of the white rings around its eyes. Babies have orange fur. 41-69cm (16-27¹/₄in) SE Asia

WHEN ....

WHERE ....

Purple-faced langur

Like all langurs, these animals are spectacular treetop acrobats. 50-65cm (19³/₄-25¹/₂in) Sri Lanka (endangered)

WHEN ....

WHERE ....

Purple-faced langur

Silvered leaf monkey

Also called a silvery lutung. This monkey uses many calls to warn, threaten, or make friends. 46-58cm (18-22³/₄in) Indonesia, Malaysia

WHEN ....

WHERE ....

François's langur

This is an agile monkey with a "peak" of fur on the top of its head. 47-64cm (18¹/₂-25in) China, Vietnam (endangered)

WHEN ....

WHERE ....

François's langur

Silvered leaf monkey

Old World: odd-nosed monkeys

Black-shanked douc

Say "dook." Look for this monkey's striking yellow eye markings and bluish face. 55-63cm (21½-24¾in) Cambodia, Vietnam (endangered)

WHEN ....

WHERE ....

Black-shanked douc

Golden snub-nosed monkey

This noisy monkey has yellow-tufted ears and a ghostly blue face. 57-76cm (22½-30in) China (endangered)

WHEN ....

WHERE ....

Golden snub-nosed monkey

Red-shanked douc

Red-shanked douc

Also called the costumed ape (although it's a monkey), because of its markings. 61-76cm (24-30in) Cambodia, Vietnam (endangered)

WHEN ....

WHERE ....

Male proboscis monkey

Female proboscis monkey, with baby

Proboscis monkey

Adult males have a dangling proboscis (another word for nose), which gives this monkey species its name. 54-76cm (21¼-30in) Borneo (endangered)

WHEN ....

WHERE ....

New World monkeys

New World monkeys live in forests in Central and South America. Their noses are flatter than those of Old World monkeys and their nostrils point to the sides. Some have flexible tails that can grip like an extra hand.

Tufted capuchin

These monkeys have a crest of long, tough hair on their forehead. 32-57cm (12½-22½in) Amazon basin

WHEN ....

WHERE ....

Tufted capuchin

Night monkey

As their name suggests, these monkeys are nocturnal – active at night. 30-42cm (12-16½in) C and S America

WHEN ....

WHERE ....

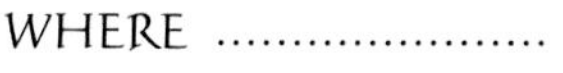

Night monkey

White-headed capuchin

White-headed capuchin

Capuchins are very intelligent, and they can even be trained to help people with disabilities. 34-45cm (13½-17¾in) C and S America

WHEN ....

WHERE ....

Squirrel monkey

Squirrel monkeys are sometimes called Death's head monkeys, because of their skull-like black and white faces. 27-35cm (10½-13¾in) S America

WHEN ....

WHERE ....

Squirrel monkey

New World: sakis and uakaris

White-faced saki

Also known as the golden-faced saki, although only males have the ring of creamy-gold facial fur. 30-35cm (12-13¾in) S America

WHEN ....

WHERE ....

White-faced saki

Bearded saki

Bearded sakis have magnificent bushy "beards" and thick tails. 40-48cm (15¾-19in) S America

WHEN ....

WHERE ....

Bearded saki

Bald-headed uakari (white)

Bald-headed uakari (red)

Bald-headed uakari

Say "wakary". These unusual monkeys have bright red faces and short tails. Their fur can be red or white. 51-56cm (20-22in) Amazon basin

WHEN ....

WHERE ....

Red titi monkeys

Red titi monkey

Titi monkeys are smaller relatives of sakis and uakaris. Male and female pairs are devoted to each other. 30-45cm (11¾-17¾in) Brazil, Peru

WHEN ....

WHERE ....

New World: marmosets

Silvery marmoset

Marmosets are tiny monkeys with claws. Look for the silvery marmoset's bare orange ears. 18-25cm (7-10in) Brazil

WHEN ....

WHERE ....

Silvery marmoset

White-fronted marmoset

Also called Geoffroy's marmoset, this monkey is easily recognized by the white fur around its face, and its black ear-tufts. Up to 20cm (8in) S America

WHEN ....

WHERE ....

White-fronted marmoset

Buffy-headed marmoset

Buffy-headed marmoset

This small monkey is so-named because of its sandy-orange head and ear tufts. 22-25cm (8½-10in) SE Brazil (endangered)

WHEN ....

WHERE ....

Pygmy marmoset

Pygmy marmoset

Also called a dwarf monkey, this tiny primate is no bigger than a guinea pig. It "talks" using trills, clicks and whistles. 12-15cm (4¾-6in) Amazon basin

WHEN ....

WHERE ....

New World: tamarins

Cotton-top tamarin

When alarmed or excited, these monkeys raise the hair on top of their head. 20cm (8in) Colombia (critically endangered)

WHEN ....

WHERE ....

Cotton-top tamarin

Golden lion tamarin

These rare monkeys have a lion-like "mane" and bright, golden coat. 26-33cm (10¼-13in) Brazil (endangered)

WHEN ....

WHERE ....

Golden lion tamarin

Emperor tamarin

The most obvious feature of this tiny monkey is its elegant, curling "moustache". 23-26cm (9-10¼in) Brazil, Peru

WHEN ....

WHERE ....

Emperor tamarin

Golden-headed lion tamarin

This monkey fluffs up its fiery orange mane and flicks out its tongue to scare enemies. Females are larger than males. 22-26cm (8½-10¼in) Brazil (endangered)

WHEN ....

WHERE ....

Golden-headed lion tamarin

Goeldi's monkey

Although sometimes called a marmoset or a tamarin, this miniature monkey is really neither. 19-23cm (7½-9in) Amazon basin

WHEN ....

WHERE ....

Goeldi's monkey

New World: spider monkeys

Geoffroy's spider monkey

Geoffroy's spider monkey

Spider monkeys have long, thin limbs, and bald ridges underneath their tails for gripping. 31-63cm (12-24¾in) C America

WHEN ....

WHERE ....

Woolly monkey

Woolly monkey

Woolly monkeys have thick, wool-like fur. Males are larger than females, and their fangs are bigger. 40-60cm (15¾-23½in) Amazon basin

WHEN ....

WHERE ....

Black howler monkey

Howler monkeys are famous for their deafening calls, which can be heard over 3km (2 miles) away. 52-71cm (20½-28in) C and S America

WHEN ....

WHERE ....

Black howler monkey

♂

♀

Woolly spider monkey

Also called muriquis, these are the largest New World monkeys. Some types have no thumbs. 55-78cm (21½-30¾in) Brazil (endangered)

WHEN ....

WHERE ....

Woolly spider monkey

Apes

Apes are the most intelligent primates. They don't have tails and they eat varied diets. There are two types: lesser apes (gibbons) and great apes, such as chimpanzees, bonobos, orangutans and gorillas.

Common chimpanzee

Chimpanzees, or chimps, are the closest living relatives of humans. They are intelligent enough to use tools, and can even learn sign language. Chimps pull faces to communicate, such as "yawning" to threaten rivals. Around 1.2m (4ft) *W* and *C* Africa (endangered)

WHEN ....

WHERE ....

Chimp using twig as tool

Frightened chimp

Excited chimp

Angry chimp

Bonobo

Bonobo

Bonobos are known for being loving, peaceful animals in the wild, unlike their more aggressive chimpanzee cousins. They are sometimes called pygmy chimpanzees, because their body shape is slimmer than a chimp's. Notice the dark face. 70-83cm (27½-32½in) DR Congo (endangered)

WHEN ....

WHERE ....

Apes: gorillas and orangutans

Western gorilla

Despite their fierce looks, these gorillas are mostly gentle fruit-eaters. Older males are called silverbacks, because the fur on their backs lightens with age. Up to 1.7m (5½ft) W Africa (critically endangered)

WHEN ....

WHERE ....

Western gorilla (silverback)

Mountain gorilla

Mountain gorilla

Mountain gorillas are slightly larger then Western gorillas, with longer fur. Only around 700 are left in the wild. Up to 1.8m (6ft) Rwanda, Uganda, DR Congo (critically endangered)

WHEN ....

WHERE ....

Bornean orangutan

Orangutans are the largest primates that live in trees, and the only great apes living wild in Asia. Up to 1.5m (4¾ft) Borneo (endangered)

WHEN ....

WHERE ....

Bornean orangutan

Sumatran orangutan

Sumatran orangutans are slightly smaller than their Bornean cousins, and even rarer. Up to 97cm (3¼ft) Sumatra (critically endangered)

WHEN ....

WHERE ....

Sumatran orangutan

Apes: gibbons

Black-crested gibbon

Pairs of black-crested gibbons sing to each other each morning with yodelling calls. 45-64cm (17¾-25in) SE Asia (critically endangered)

WHEN ....

WHERE ....

Black-crested gibbon

Siamang gibbon

Siamang gibbon

These are the biggest and loudest of the gibbons. Look for their inflatable throat pouch. Up to 1m (3¼ft) SE Asia (endangered)

WHEN ....

WHERE ....

Pileated gibbon

Like the black-crested gibbon, males and females of this species have different markings. Gibbons usually swing through trees, but can walk upright too. 43-60cm (17-23½in) SE Asia (endangered)

WHEN ....

WHERE ....

Pileated gibbon

Lar gibbon

Lar gibbon

Lar gibbons come in many shades, but all have white fur around their faces. 45-58cm (17¾-23in) SE Asia (endangered)

WHEN ....

WHERE ....

Prosimians

Prosimians, such as lemurs and bush babies, are relatives of monkeys and apes. Like all primates, they can use their hands to grasp.

Ring-tailed lemur

Ring-tailed lemur

Ring-tailed lemurs are often seen in zoos. They live in large groups, led by females. 39-46cm (15½-18in) Madagascar

WHEN ....

WHERE ....

Greater bamboo lemur

Greater bamboo lemur

As their name suggests, these lemurs live in bamboo forests. 28-45cm (11-17¾in) Madagascar (critically endangered)

WHEN ....

WHERE ....

Ruffed lemur

Ruffed lemur

This is the largest type of lemur. Like most lemurs, it grooms itself using its comb-like teeth. Up to 53cm (21in) Madagascar (critically endangered)

WHEN ....

WHERE ....

Sclater's lemur

This is one of the very few primates that have blue eyes. Males are black, females are reddish-brown. 39-45cm (15½-17¾in) Madagascar (endangered)

WHEN ....

WHERE ....

Sclater's lemur ♂

Prosimians: more lemurs

Pygmy mouse lemur

Pygmy mouse lemur

This mini primate can go into a coma-like state called a torpor to save energy. 6-8cm (2½-3in) Madagascar

WHEN ....

WHERE ....

Goodman's mouse lemur

Like cats, mouse lemurs have a shiny layer inside their eyes which helps them to see well in the dark. Up to 9.5cm (3¾in) Madagascar

WHEN ....

WHERE ....

Goodman's mouse lemur

Berthe's mouse lemur

Berthe's mouse lemur

Believed to be the world's smallest primate, this tiny lemur has bare fingers and large eyes. Up to 9cm (3½in) Madagascar (endangered)

WHEN ....

WHERE ....

Fat-tailed dwarf lemur

Fat-tailed dwarf lemur

Like hedgehogs, these lemurs hibernate in winter, living off fat stored in their chunky tails. Up to 20cm (8in) Madagascar

WHEN ....

WHERE ....

Fork-marked lemur

Fork-marked lemurs feed mostly on sticky gum under tree bark, scraping it out with their teeth. 23-28cm (9-11in) Madagascar

WHEN ....

WHERE ....

Fork-marked lemur

Indri

Indris are a type of large lemur. They are known for their loud, wailing songs. Unlike other lemurs, they have stubby tails. 64-72cm (25¼-28¼ft) Madagascar (endangered)

WHEN ....

WHERE ....

Indri

Woolly lemur

Woolly lemur

Also known as avahis, woolly lemurs eat mostly leaves and take long naps while they digest their food. 26-30cm (10¼-11¾in) Madagascar

WHEN ....

WHERE ....

Diademed sifaka

Diademed sifaka

Sifakas are named because of their harsh "shii-fark" call. A diadem is a type of crown, which refers to the "crown" of white fur around this lemur's face. 50-55cm (19¾-21½in) Madagascar (endangered)

WHEN ....

WHERE ....

Aye-aye

Silky sifaka

These rare, elegant animals have soft white fur and a bare face. Only 250 or so are left in the wild. 48-54cm (19-21¼in) Madagascar (critically endangered)

WHEN ....

WHERE ....

Silky sifaka

Aye-aye

Despite its rat-like teeth, bat-like ears and skunk-like tail, an aye-aye is a type of lemur. Look for its long, twig-like middle finger. 44-53cm (17¼-21in) Madagascar

WHEN ....

WHERE ....

Prosimians: lorises and pottos

Slender loris

Lorises are small, nocturnal animals with long, skinny limbs and huge, round eyes for seeing in the dark. They mainly eat bugs, often kinds that are dangerous to other animals. 15-25cm (6-10in) India, Sri Lanka

WHEN ....

WHERE ....

Slender loris

Potto

A potto marks its territory with a curry-like scent that comes from glands under its tail. The first finger on each of its hands is only a tiny stub. 30-40cm ($11\frac{3}{4}$-$15\frac{3}{4}$in) W and C Africa

WHEN ....

WHERE ....

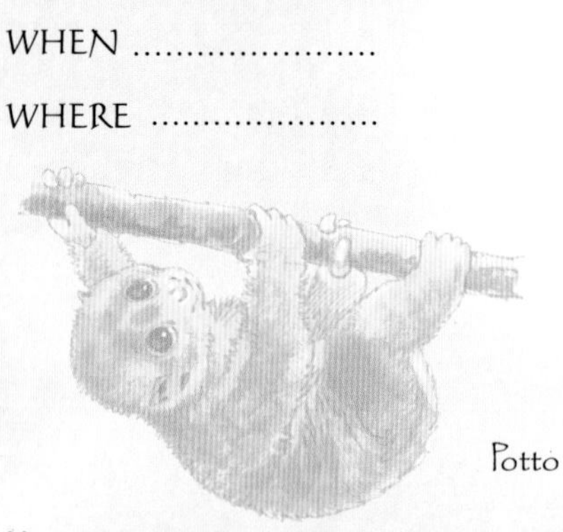

Potto

Slow loris

Slow loris

These animals have flexible bodies and an excellent grip. They move slowly, but can make venom to spit on any attackers. 21-38cm ($8\frac{1}{4}$-15in) SE Asia

WHEN ....

WHERE ....

Golden angwantibo

Golden angwantibo

This type of potto is sometimes called a bear monkey because of its round ears. Like lorises, angwantibos have tiny tails. 22-30cm ($8\frac{1}{2}$-12in) C Africa

WHEN ....

WHERE ....

Prosimians: bush babies

Southern lesser galago

Galagos – also known as bush babies – are incredible leapers, reaching up to 2m (6½ft) with each jump. They can turn their heads 180 degrees to see behind them, like an owl. 14-17cm (5½-6¾in) S Africa

WHEN ....

WHERE ....

Southern lesser galago

Greater galago

These are the largest galagos. They are also known as thick-tailed greater galagos, because of their bushy tails. 25-40cm (10-15¾in) C and S Africa

WHEN ....

WHERE ....

Greater galago

Demidoff's galago

Demidoff's galago

Also known as a dwarf bush baby, this is the smallest type of galago. Its eyes don't move, but its huge ears can swivel to hear sounds from all around. 7-15cm (2¾-6in) W and C Africa

WHEN ....

WHERE ....

Philippine tarsier

Philippine tarsier

A tarsier is a unique type of primate that isn't a monkey, ape or prosimian. Tarsiers have huge eyes – each one is as big as their brain. 10-14cm (4-5½in) Philippines

WHEN ....

WHERE ....

Index

Sticker numbers are in brackets.

Designed by Reuben Barrance
Consultant: Twycross Zoo – East Midland Zoological Society, UK
Edited by Kirsteen Rogers
Cover designed by Michael Hill

Cover images © NHPA/Gerald Cubitt
First published in 2011 by Usborne Publishing Ltd., 83–85 Saffron Hill, London EC1N 8RT, England.

First published in America 2011. UE. Printed in Heshan, Guangdong, China.